MY BLUE HAIKU

MY BLUE HAIKU

~A Collection of Poems~

SONYA LEWIS

To the ones who are blue in the
sun and in the rain

This beautiful blue book is dedicated to Lhayelle, Latoya, and Lhayana; without whom there is no me; you are my world and I love you!   To Freddie and Anne, you are so greatly loved and missed. To Freddie, Jr., you showed me how to live life to the fullest; Thank you, I love you! To Javan, my inspiration! This is my "Alchemy" baby! I love you!

CONTENTS

On Lessons (love) learned

I bask in your love
And pray for the grace to stay
Your world is too hard

~ Narcissist's no love

You leave such a small
Window for me to climb into
Too busy

~ make time for me

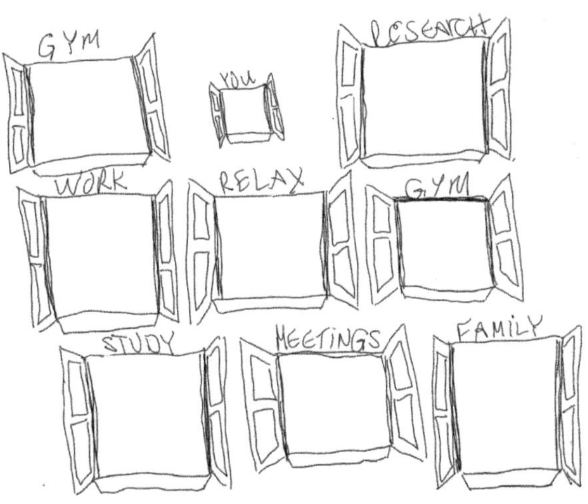

My heart calls to you
You let me down so fiercely
My ego is bruised

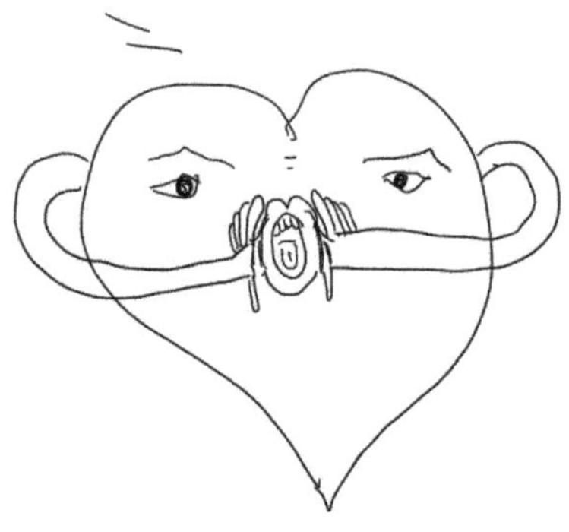

I bought all the food
I thought I was invited
You had other plans

~ the cookout

He ushered in the pain
Now I usher in the rain
And wash out the mud

Your idea of space
Is finding love somewhere else
Behind the closed doors

~ the affair

Irreplaceable
Your love Undeniable
Why can't I feel it?

Why do we pretend
To let one another in
When we both have walls?

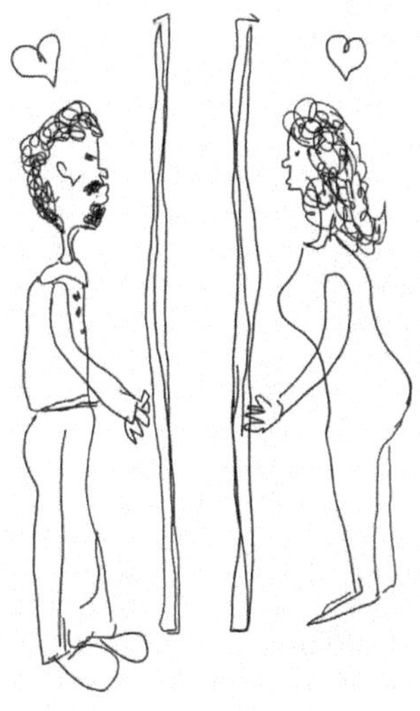

No one will EVER
Love you like I did NO ONE
Will bring life to you

~ embracing my worth

Why can't we be US?
Strolling happily through life
No cares to bother

~ Him

I don't feel special
I await your messages
You do not respond

~ ghosted

There was a long bridge
I traveled across for you
You dissipated

~ meet me halfway

How can I move on?
When you're still holding the key
That unlocks my door

~ Narcissist hold

I found heart pieces
While rummaging through your shit
Buried deep in the crevices

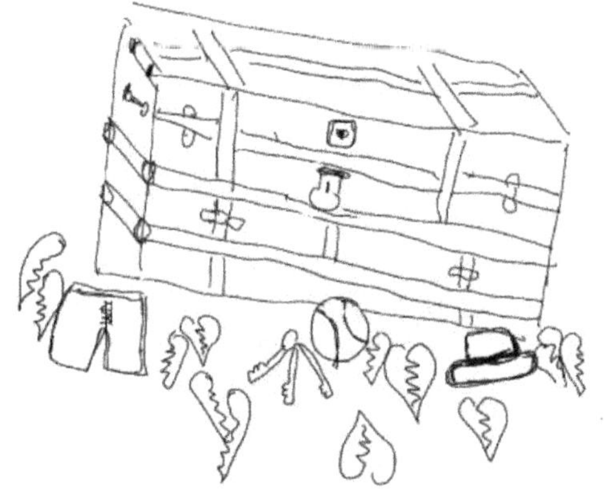

15

Many days go by
You made promises to me
I am still waiting

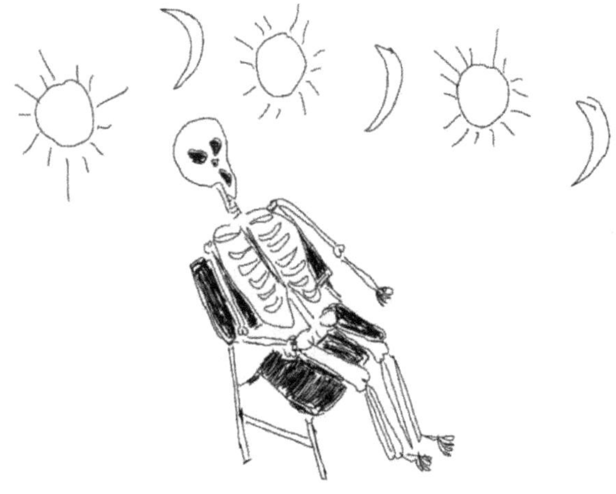

You are a mountain
I climbed to the highest point
Then you pushed me off

- I put you on a pedestal

Why didn't you say
What you were really feeling?
I would have listened

On our way to town
Your harsh words made my face frown
I want to go home

~ one of many one-way arguments

The fork in the road
Led me to you, but you left
Before I arrived

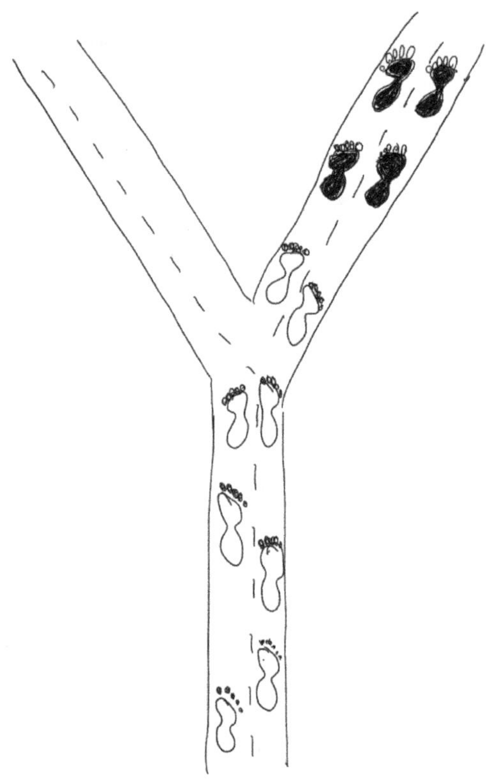

Love wears a disguise
When I look into your eyes
Chivalry has died

Your kiss was so sweet
I imagined it would be
It never happened

- never been kissed

If chances were one
I'd want one more than I have
Look at me again

- the one I never got to know

My words cut you deep
Now I can hardly stand sleep
Please come back to me

You saw me slightly
Leaned in and gave me your all
Seeing me no more

I'm homeless
You closed the door
To the only home I knew

- my heart has no home

When a man takes a woman's flower,
It's him ceasing power
That's his only defense

Forgotten
Hypnotism performed, No
Memories of you left behind

~ I've moved on

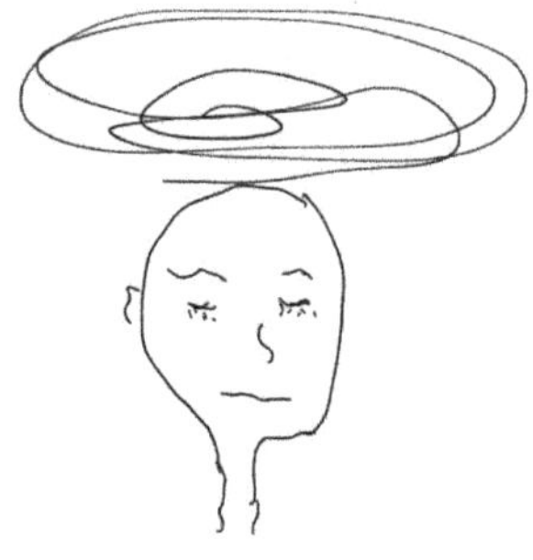

The carcass of the soul you killed
Lay lifeless at your feet
I walk over it, stepping out of my skin
Into a new and improved me

I wish I knew
I wish I could know
I wish you would say
Was it just a one-night stand?
I will never know

I let down a lot of walls with you
Tumbling my heavily guarded
Safe space to the ground

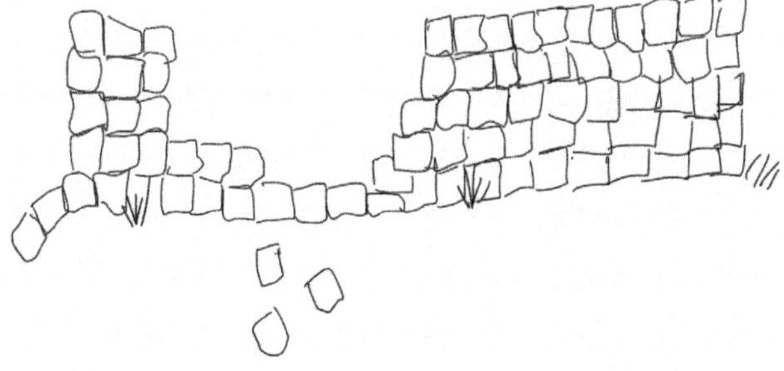

Yeah, it's me
The person you said you couldn't resist
Now I don't exist

You ask me to run
Then refuse to run with me
Basking in the sun

My joy lies in you
I give you my whole heart
That is the mistake

~ that time I loved too much

Inside, you find out
Open the door and walk out
Never to return

Music stole my soul
You were music to my ears
Broken records lie

I can't help myself
I crowd my mind with your name
You're the one I blame

Manipulation
Continued exploitation
Barely escaping

The first love I knew
Was a love which did not last
Slowly it past fast

SECTION TWO

On Loss

You were a true friend
You saved me from destruction
I want you alive

~ I am eternally grateful for you

42

Should I mourn or hope?
Should I cry or laugh with joy?
Should I sit and wait?

- show me a sign

To live is to dream
To sail was your "Alchemy"
It took you away

- for Jovan

The hole is so big
Not even love can fill it
Huge significance

~ missing my friend ☹

Were the two men thieves?
Did they rob you and steal your boat?
Let me hear your voice

~seeking answers

I miss you I miss
You I miss you I miss you
I miss you I miss

Don't call off the search
I want to keep on looking
Check beneath the tree
(Check beneath the sea)

The Oceans' waves thrashed
I heard your voice but no more
The sea shed its tears

~ J.P.

Throw out the Lifeline
A wounded heart needs saving
Stitches won't heal me

~ grieving the moments, we are missing

You lived your life loud
You left a huge impression
The memories stuck

Thanks for saving me
From a life of misery
I thought I was lost

SECTION THREE

On Love

The hot tea boils
You wait in the room asleep
Let love spill all over

If the rain would stop
All that we know would dry up
Let it rain non-stop

Your river, my stream
The fulfillment of a dream
We collide in space

I think we have something here
Or is it just my imagination?
I could easily walk away
But is that really what you want?

I want you, you said
Like dry crops thirst for water
Then you flowed on me

Love is all I need
The world can spin forever
Love is all I breathe

How much do I love?
If you count, one million ways
Will not be enough

You make my song sing
The lyrics and melodies
Your sweet sunshine brings

I don't know if I
have half of a chance with you
But I know, I'd like it if I did

~ Sweden

Your body wrapped mine
Morphing into one being
We spoon

If you call on me
I promise I will be there
Even if you aren't

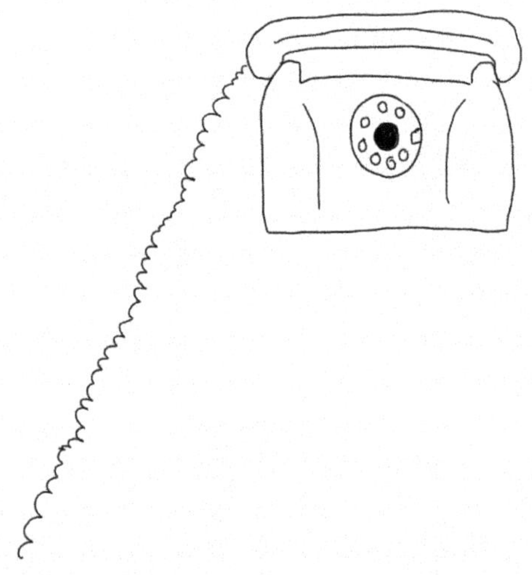

Are You my true blue?
Imaginary new blue?
Virtually you

~ For N

Truth is relative
Love is inevitable
You are all I know

The laughter of kids
The dogs barking in the yard
The white picket fences

~ our world

I try to resist
Your sweet taste between my lips
Forces indulgence

~ temptation

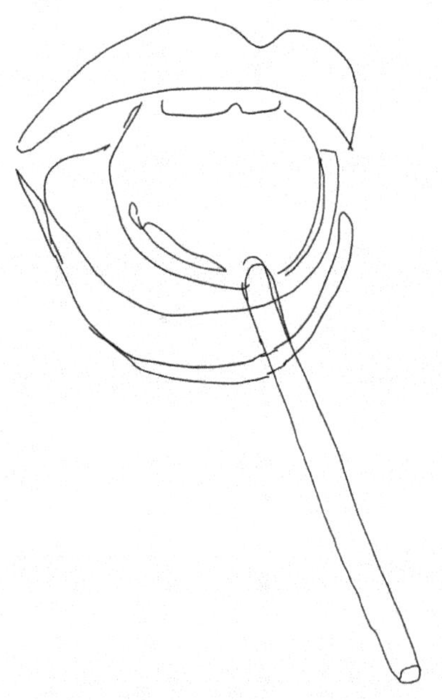

Your love flows through me
Your water quenches my thirst
I am satisfied

My head on your chest
Your scruff beard rubbing my hair
We were so close then

Your shirt, shoes, and socks
Lying on the bedroom floor
A man is present

Long walks in the park
The pigeons sit on the bench
Beside us, we're chill

Glass of lemonade
Porch with 2 rocking chairs
Watching the sunset

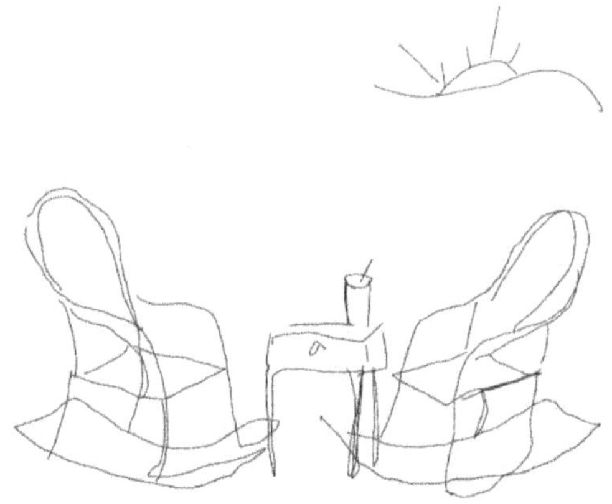

Your love took over
Ushering me into bliss
How could I resist?

The forbidden place
We lay in each other's arms
I will remember

- *Albania*

Can we learn to love?
Each other like we used to
I really miss us

If you take me out
I will make it worth your while
It's not what you think

My heart belongs to
All the You(s) there will ever be
From now until eternity

~ the One

You can't imagine
Just how happy it makes me
When I hear your voice

~ sweet, sweet Sweden

Your eyes are so blue
I'm lost in the sea of you
Your waves engulf me

~ lost in the sea of N

I awake and wait
You are cause to celebrate
My day is now clear

~ possibility of new love

You are my new b(l)oo
I yearn to discover you
Let the love ensue

~ *Salkin*

Summer skies peep through
Blue is the color of love
Your rays cool me down

Even though you know
What you don't know, won't hurt you
I won't keep secrets

Your love sustains me
Food and water I give up
I eat and drink you

SECTION FOUR

On Life

What I see in you
I want you to see in you
Phenomenally

~ believe in yourself

You cannot deny
You have the potential to
Fly like a bird high

The sun met the moon
Together they shined brighter
Oh! What two can do

~ teamwork

The struggle to win
When everything around you
Says you stand to lose

- persevere even when the odds are against you

If words could talk what
Would your words say to the world?
Would they change anything?

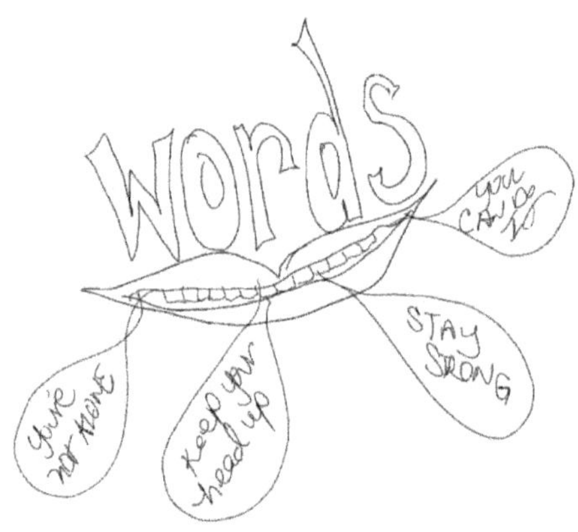

The wind screamed my name
I am a step out of time
Lead me to my path

~ trying to find my place in this world

The flowers are ripe
During your walk, stop and smell
They leave with Winter

My life is a square
I keep bumping the corners
Help me smooth them out

- it's ok to talk to someone

The road leads to joy
The train is at the station
Hop on while you can

The sun is shining
The sky is so blue tonight
The stars are on fire

You are in control
Your future is in your hands
Build a ship and sail

The borders are closed
Who could have imagined it?
Making history

~ covid19

The climate is cold
Nothing is to be trusted
Keep your eyes open

~ pandemic policy

Nice shiny new car
Red is my favorite color
Can I have a ride?

Lonely birds flying
Trying to find their next prey
Will they land on you?

Let go of the past
The past will let go of you
Then you can be free

103

There is a green place
I want to find where it is
Will I belong there?

- in search of purpose

Empty feelings come
Empty feelings go away
Don't ever come back

With wings you blossom
You fly higher than you knew
You have so much strength

Metamorphosis
Emerge better than you were
Your colors are bright

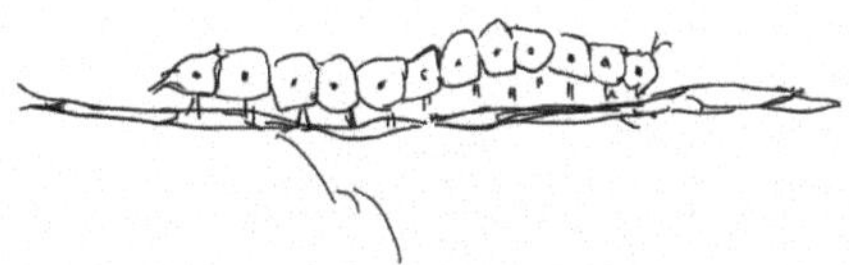

The secret to life
Is to not ever look back
Keep your head intact

Let me grab a bus
Travel the world with a smile
Be back in a while

I wish to tell you
About life, love, and freedom
This is all you need

Your waves knocked me down
But they could not consume me
An angel appeared

~ Rehoboth Beach

The journey is long
You my friend are not alone
Never be afraid

Age does not matter
You can achieve what you want
Push through the bias

They tell me to stop
I tell me to go faster
Listen to your own voice

I managed to fly
Even with the sky so high
I just float on clouds

How Magnificent
The world cannot contain you
You are powerful

Birds land on your limbs
The sun beams bright from above
The rain showers you

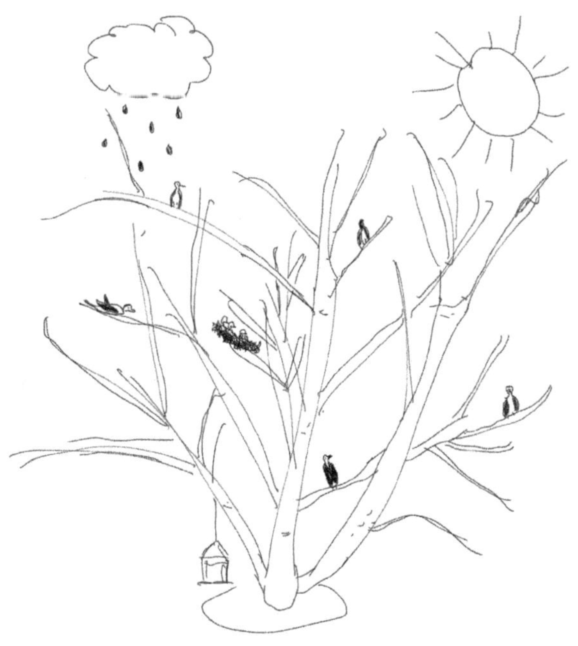

Helicopters cross
Paths with jets in the blue sky
Destiny fuels you

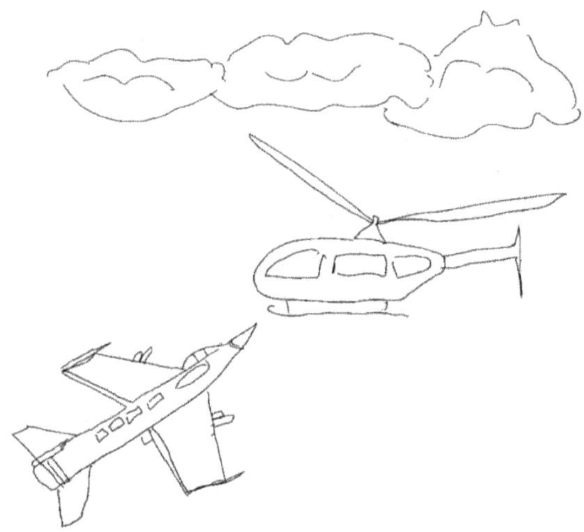

The clouds form faces
They part and give way to light
Feel the energy

The fruit tree bore fruit
The squirrels ate the fallen crop
The earth feeds its prey

The swift grey rabbit
Ran across my lawn in fear
Was there a fox nearby?

I am not my skin
We can help each other win
Focus on within

~ be everybody's keeper

The lighthouse at sea
Sends out a signal to me
Run the other way

- *listen to your inner voice*

Fear knocked down my door
Without needing permission
Leaving me helpless

- anxiety

Emerge from ashes
Phoenix rising to the top
No one can hold you

I can't see myself
Outside of this body I
Have grown accustomed to

~ weight gain

To live without fear
Is my greatest hope and prayer
Breathing the air of freedom

~ seeing myself beyond anxiety

The fear took over
And all sense of hope was gone
Paralysis won

Stand beneath the tree
It bears fruit that you can't see
It's the giving tree

Imagine your Dream
Put yourself fully in it
Now live your best life

DREAM

FLY

SOAR

Be strong, Be fearless
Be the best You, you can be
We will meet again

The Beginning...

Now starts your literary Journey! Write!

Write

Write

Write

Write

Write

CPSIA information can be obtained
at www.ICGtesting.com
Printed in the USA
BVHW081510170522
637235BV00008B/587